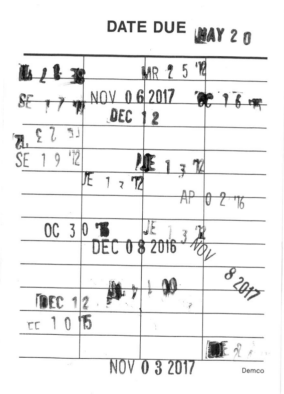

DATE DUE MAY 2 0

JL 28	MR 2 5 '12	
SE 17	NOV 0 6 2017	OC 16
	DEC 1 2	
JL 23		
SE 1 9 '12	JE 1 3 '12	
	JE 1 3 72	AP 0 2 '16
OC 3 0 '13	JE 1 3 72	NOV
	DEC 0 8 2016	8 2017
DEC 1 2	JU 7 1 00	
FE 1 0 15		
		JE 2

NOV 0 3 2017   Demco

AMERICAN HUMANE

Protecting Children & Animals Since 1877

THE LEARNING RESOURCE CENTER
Weston Intermediate School

Beginning Pet Care
WITH AMERICAN HUMANE

Learning to Care for a
DOG

Felicia Lowenstein Niven

Bailey Books
an imprint of
Enslow Publishers, Inc.
40 Industrial Road
Box 398
Berkeley Heights, NJ 07922
USA
http://www.enslow.com

AMERICAN HUMANE

Protecting Children & Animals Since 1877

Founded in 1877, the American Humane Association is the only national organization dedicated to protecting both children and animals. Through a network of child and animal protection agencies and individuals, American Humane develops policies, legislation, curricula, and training programs — and takes action — to protect children and animals from abuse, neglect, and exploitation. To learn how you can support American Humane's vision of a nation where no child or animal will ever be a victim of abuse or neglect, visit www.americanhumane. org, phone (303) 792-9900, or write to the American Humane Association at 63 Inverness Drive East, Englewood, Colorado, 80112-5117.

To our Readers:

We have done our best to make sure all Internet Addresses in this book were active and appropriate when we went to press. However, the author and the publisher have no control over and assume no liability for the material available on those Internet sites or on other Web sites they may link to. Any comments or suggestions can be sent by e-mail to comments@enslow.com or to the address on the back cover.

Every effort has been made to locate all copyright holders of material used in this book. If any errors or omissions have occurred, corrections will be made in future editions of this book.

To Adina and Shayna (personal fairy godmothers to rescue dogs) —May your magic continue to make a difference.

Bailey Books, an imprint of Enslow Publishers, Inc.

Copyright © 2011 by Enslow Publishers, Inc.

Library of Congress Cataloging-in-Publication Data

Niven, Felicia Lowenstein.
  Learning to care for a dog / Felicia Lowenstein Niven.
      p. cm. — (Beginning pet care with American Humane)
  Includes bibliographical references and index.
  Summary: "Readers will learn how to choose, train, and care for a dog"—Provided by publisher.
  ISBN 978-0-7660-3190-6
  1. Dogs—Juvenile literature. I. Title.
  SF426.5.N58 2010
  636.7—dc22
                                                2008048962

Printed in China

052010 Leo Paper Group, Heshan City, Guangdong, China

10 9 8 7 6 5 4 3 2 1

Illustration Credits: All animals in logo bar and boxes, Shutterstock. Associated Press, pp. 19, 25, 42; © 2010 Clipart.com, a division of Getty Images, p. 13; Courtesy of http://Dogs.TheFunTimesGuide.com, p. 29; Lee Celano/WireImage, p. 43; Masterfile, pp. 3 (thumbnail 4), 24, 30, 40; Nancy Fantuzzi, pp. 3 (thumbnails 1, 2), 4, 5, 6, 9, 10; Official White House Photo by Chuck Kennedy, p. 41; Shutterstock, pp. 1, 3, (thumbnails 3, 5, 6)11, 14, 15, 20, 21, 22, 23 (all), 28, 33, 37, 39, 43; Victor Englebert/Photo Researchers, Inc., p. 26; © Werner Layer/Animals Animals-Earth Sciences, p. 16.

Cover Illustration: Shutterstock (golden retriever puppy).

Table of Contents

Chapter 1
Rescue

Abby was frozen with fear. She stood with her tail between her legs, shivering. This mixed-breed dog had come from a place where people treated her poorly. In this new home, she did not know what to expect.

Nancy Fantuzzi knew just what to do. As a member of Rogers Rescues, she works with many kinds of dogs. She helps them get ready to be adopted.

Rescue

Abby was lucky to be rescued!

Nancy got her laptop. She sat on the floor away from Abby. Nancy worked while the dog watched, but Abby did not try to come near. This went on for about a week.

Then one day, Nancy was surprised. Abby walked right up to her and sniffed. Nancy's heart jumped for joy. She reached out to pet the dog. Abby let her!

Nancy worked with Abby until the dog was comfortable with her.

Rescue

But the dog still had a long way to go. She was okay with Nancy but scared of everybody else. She could not even go for a walk outside.

Nancy was able to hook the leash to her collar.

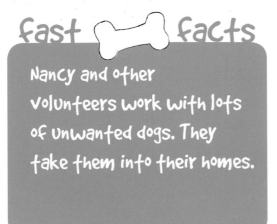

fast facts

Nancy and other volunteers work with lots of unwanted dogs. They take them into their homes.

But as soon as they stepped outside, Abby flattened to the ground. She would not go another step.

Nancy kept trying. After a week, they got as far as the end of the driveway. But then, Abby saw a strange man. She ran back into the house. They had to start all over again.

It took months before Abby felt comfortable. Still Nancy was not sure that anyone would want to adopt such a timid dog. Then she got a phone call. A woman wanted a friend for her other shy dog.

Rescue

The woman came to visit Abby several times. It was a perfect match. In a few weeks, Abby joined her new family.

Today, Abby is a more confident dog. She goes canoeing and hiking. She competes in agility, an obstacle course for dogs. It would never have happened without groups like Rogers Rescues.

Nancy and other volunteers work with lots of unwanted dogs. They take them into their homes. They get to know the animals. Then, they find the right families to adopt them.

Sometimes the dogs have special problems. Cody only had three legs. A car had hit him. At first, he had some trouble getting around. But he learned quickly. Now he goes to work with his new owner. He sits in her quilt shop and greets everyone.

Jack also had just three legs. That did not stop him from jumping on the bed. People saw that he was a normal dog. He got adopted, too.

Cody was rescued, then adopted into a great family.

Rescue

Said Nancy, "Dogs like Abby, Jack, and Cody teach us that we can overcome anything!"

There are many reasons that people adopt dogs. Sometimes they want a dog to protect them. They may want to exercise with a dog. Plus, dogs are good friends. They are always happy to see us.

Dogs also are a great responsibility. In the following pages, you will learn more about what it means to own and care for a dog.

Jack has only three legs, but that didn't stop him from being adopted.

Chapter 2
History of the Dog

It may be hard to believe, but there was a time when there were no dogs. This was about 100,000 years ago. Some scientists believe that around this time man probably took home some wolf pups. Humans raised these pups. The pups learned to hunt with the men.

History of the Dog

They ate scraps from meals. They helped warn humans when other animals were around.

We know that cavemen had dogs. We see them in early cave drawings. We know that people in ancient Egypt and China had dogs, too. Dogs appear in their sculptures and art. In fact, the Egyptians worshipped dogs. In China, tiny dogs were used to keep people warm. They hid in people's wide sleeves!

Humans began to breed dogs for certain characteristics. Some people wanted dogs with a good sense of smell. They could help in hunting. Others wanted dogs that were smaller. They could fit in spaces where rats and other pests lived. They could help keep them out of homes and gardens.

Today, there are many different kinds of dogs. These include dogs that are bred with the special traits needed to rescue people. There are "seeing eye" dogs to help the blind. There are guard dogs to

History of the Dog

Dogs and people learned to live with each other more than 14,000 years ago. Pictures of dogs have been found on walls in ancient tombs in Egypt.

protect people and places. There are herding dogs to keep sheep and cattle together. There are dogs that keep us company. But they all share one thing in common. Dogs are our special friends.

Chapter 3
Getting a Dog

Dogs come in all colors and sizes. Some are purebred. There are more than 150 breeds recognized by the American Kennel Club, from the tiny Chihuahua to the Great Dane. Others are mixed breeds. Their mother and father may be two different purebreds or a mix of breeds.

Whether you choose a mixed breed or purebred, finding the right dog for your family is very important. If you do not find a good match, there could be a lot of problems.

14

Getting a Dog

Where do you live? You want to match the size of the dog to your home. If you live in an apartment, look for a small dog that does not need a lot of exercise. If you have a large home and a fenced backyard, you may have the right space for a larger dog.

Size alone does not determine the best fit. Consider the activity level. Some breeds are more active than others. For example, border collies are bred to herd sheep. They are very active.

Dogs come in all sizes! This huge Great Dane is sniffing a Chihuahua.

Getting a Dog

They will be bored if you do not give them lots of exercise. That could lead to behavior problems.

The Newfoundland is less active. This breed might be a better choice if you want a big dog that is calmer.

Some breeds are better with children than others. A child's rough play might be too much for a Yorkshire terrier. An easily excited breed, like an Irish setter or terrier, might have too much energy for a young child.

Another thing to consider is shedding. Some dogs shed more than others. You might not mind if a dog

Newfoundlands are big dogs, but may be calmer than other dog breeds.

Getting a Dog

sheds, but having to clean up all that hair might be a problem.

Even if you are getting a mixed breed, it is good to know about the purebred dogs. Dogs that are mixes of these breeds will have traits of their parents or grandparents.

Once you decide on the kind of dog, you have one more decision to make. Will you get a puppy or an adult? A puppy is more work. However, you can train a puppy the way that you like. Adult dogs are often house-trained, but you might also have to break them of some bad habits.

There are several places to get a dog. You can find dogs at your local animal shelter. At shelters, there are usually many types of adult dogs and puppies. There are some purebreds and some mixed breeds.

If you want a particular breed of dog, you may want to contact a breed rescue group. These groups have just one type of purebred for adoption.

Getting a Dog

For example, a golden retriever rescue will have only golden retrievers. Most of the dogs from breed rescues are adult dogs that have lost their homes.

The cost to adopt a dog from a shelter or breed rescue group is usually low. These places charge a fee just to cover their costs in caring for the dogs while they are looking for a good home.

If you want a purebred puppy and you are willing to spend more money, you can buy one from a breeder. Breeders raise dogs of a certain type. You can usually meet the puppy's parents. That way you can know how the dog might turn out.

Pet shops also sell puppies. Sometimes the animals at pet shops are treated well, but sometimes they are not. Wherever you go to find your dog, look around and pay attention. Is the place clean? Are the dogs healthy? Ask a lot of questions. Make sure you are getting a healthy dog.

It is a good idea to have your new dog checked out by a veterinarian (vet). You can find one in your

Getting a Dog

local telephone yellow pages. You may also want to ask friends or neighbors for recommendations.

Make an appointment with your vet as soon as you can. A new puppy will need several visits the first year. Adult dogs usually need just one visit each year, unless they get sick.

Animal shelters and rescue groups often have adoption days at pet stores. Check out your local pet store to see if they have adoption days!

Getting a Dog

On the first visit, the vet will examine your dog. He will weigh your dog and take his temperature. The vet will look for fleas or other parasites. If vaccines are needed, he will give those shots.

The vet may also test your dog for heartworm disease. This is a disease that can kill dogs. But it is completely preventable. Your vet will send medicine home with you. You will need to remember to give your dog the heartworm medication once a month to keep him healthy.

Best of all, the vet can answer your questions. Write them down so you do not forget what you want to know.

Do you want a puppy or an adult dog? Talk with your family and choose the right kind of dog that will be best for your family.

Take your new pet to the vet right away. The vet will also answer any questions you may have.

Chapter 4
Health and Exercise

When your parents bring a new baby into the house, they buy bottles and diapers. When you get a dog, you need the right supplies, too.

A leash, collar, and dog bowls are a good start. Dog beds and crates are places for dogs to rest. Gates and fences help keep them safe. Brushes and nail clippers are useful for grooming.

Health and Exercise

Every dog needs a collar, leash, and food and water bowls.

Some people also buy dog shampoo and toothpaste. These are different from the shampoo and toothpaste that people use. Dog shampoo is specially made for a dog's skin. Dog toothpaste is made from ingredients that are safe for dogs to swallow. It has a taste that they like. Of course, you do not have to wash your dog at home. You can take your dog to a groomer for baths and teeth cleaning.

Some people like giving their dogs baths at home. Others prefer going to a groomer.

Dogs also enjoy toys, balls, biscuits, and chew toys. These keep them entertained. Some dog biscuits and chew toys also help to keep their teeth clean.

But dog biscuits and treats are not the same as food. You will have to keep a steady supply of dog food on hand. You can choose dry or wet food.

Health and Exercise

Your vet can recommend a good brand and how much to feed your dog.

You may decide to give your dog some human food, too. Be careful. It is not always good for your pet. For example, chocolate can be poisonous, and some other foods can be unhealthy, too. Check with your vet to find out what is best for your dog.

Those are the basic supplies. But that is not the end of the list.

Make sure your dog always wears a collar and an identification (ID) tag with your address and phone number. This way, if your dog gets lost, someone who finds your dog can also find you.

Microchips are tiny computer chips. The vet places the microchip under your pet's skin.

Health and Exercise

A microchip is another way to identify your dog. Your vet injects the microchip under the skin of your pet. This type of ID is always with your dog. Each of these tiny computer chips has its own special code. If someone finds your dog, he or she can have the dog scanned by a veterinarian or an animal shelter. The microchip's special code will come up on the scanner and then the person will be able to find you.

Most cities and towns require that dogs be licensed. You will need to fill out a form and pay a small fee. You will also have to show that your dog

Once you have a leash and collar, you can take your dog for walks!

has had all of her shots. Then the city clerk will give you a license tag for your dog to wear.

Now that your dog has a leash and collar with tags, you are ready to go outside. You can take your dog for a walk. You can play fetch. You can let your dog run around in the backyard. All dogs need exercise every day to stay healthy.

Usually, dogs adopted from an animal shelter or breed rescue are already spayed or neutered. If you get a dog or puppy that has not been spayed or neutered, you should consider having this done. You will be helping to control pet overpopulation and will be giving your dog a healthier life.

Spaying and neutering are operations that prevent animals from having babies. It is called spaying for a female and neutering for a male. These operations are done by your veterinarian. Spaying or neutering your dog can make her or him healthier by preventing some types of diseases. Dogs that are spayed or neutered are also not as likely to run away or get lost.

Chapter 5

Problems and Challenges

Owning a dog is fun. It is also challenging. You may face some problems. Knowing about them will help.

Do you have a puppy?

You must "puppy proof" your home. Young dogs are very active. They like to explore everywhere. They also like to chew. It helps their mouths feel better when new teeth are coming in.

Make sure dangerous materials are out of reach.

Problems and Challenges

A puppy could chew or swallow wires, crayons, paper clips, pins, staples, and coins. Even some houseplants are poisonous.

A crate is a place where you dog can sleep and eat.

When your puppy is not in a safe area, you may want to keep him in a crate. A crate is used for dogs of all ages. Some crates have metal sides like a cage. Other crates have soft sides. Dogs think of it as a bed or safe place to relax.

House-training your new pet is hard work, but with patience your dog will soon be going to the bathroom outside.

Problems and Challenges

Crates can be helpful when you are ready to house-train your dog. House-training is teaching your dog to go to the bathroom outside. Dogs usually will not go to the bathroom in their crate. That is where they rest and sleep.

Puppies need to go to the bathroom very often. Adult dogs can wait longer. You will get to know your dog's bathroom habits. When you take your dog out of the crate, it is a good time for a bathroom break. Take your dog outside when he wakes up and before he goes to bed. Bring him outside fifteen to thirty minutes after each meal. Take him outside several times a day.

Watch his behavior. If you see him sniffing the carpet or floor, it might be time to go outside. Praise your dog every time he goes to the bathroom in the right place. Praise is important. Never punish a dog for making a mistake. If your dog has an accident in the house, correct him with a firm, "No." Then take the dog outside right away to show him the right place. Praise him there.

Problems and Challenges

House-training is one challenge. Here are some other common problems.

Play Biting

Puppies play by using their sharp little teeth. But they need to learn that they cannot play that way with people.

When your puppy nips you in play, let her know it hurts. Make a loud squeal. Stop playing. Leave the puppy alone. Do not give her any attention. Then, after a few minutes, try again. The puppy will learn that biting causes the play to stop.

Digging

Some dogs like to dig. They may dig for fun. They may also dig to escape, for shelter, or to find small animals.

Find out the reason your dog digs. If she needs shelter, you can provide a doghouse. If she digs for fun, maybe more toys will help. If she is trying to escape, you can block the area under your fence with rocks or chicken wire.

If digging continues to be a problem, call a dog trainer. You can also keep your dog inside more often.

When your dog chews something he shouldn't, give him a chew toy that he can chew on. Make sure to pick the right kind of chew toy for your dog.

Problems and Challenges

Barking

You expect dogs to bark. But some dogs bark a lot.

There are many reasons that dogs bark. It could be because they are lonely or bored. They bark because they are guarding their space. They sometimes bark because they are scared. You have to be a detective to figure out why they bark. Then you can help them to stop.

One way to stop barking is to teach a quiet command. When your dog barks, say "Quiet." Then, shake a can of pennies. The noise will surprise him. He will likely stop barking for a moment. Praise him and give him a treat. Repeat as often as you can until your dog understands the meaning of the command. Then you will no longer need the can.

If a dog barks out of fear, you may need to do something else. Discover what scares your dog.

For example, it could be a loud noise. Allow him to experience that noise in a softer tone. Then slowly increase the volume.

Dog trainers are skilled in problems such as these. You may want to ask a trainer for help.

Pulling on the Leash

Some dogs pull when walked on a leash. This is not fun for you. It also can be dangerous if you cannot control your dog.

Training can help. Keep the leash loose. As soon as the leash straightens, stop. When your dog turns around to see what happened, praise her. You can give her a treat if you would like. Start walking again and repeat the behavior. Some trainers will not just stop; they will walk in the opposite direction.

Another way to stop pulling is to buy a head collar. These collars prevent dogs from pulling. Get one fitted for your dog at your local pet store.

Accidents

Even after they are house-trained, some dogs urinate, or "pee," inside. They may do this when they are very excited. Sometimes it happens when they are scared. Male dogs may even do it to mark their spot.

Do not punish a dog for this type of behavior. It might make it worse. Instead, take your dog outside as much as possible. Try not to surprise your dog. That could help. Remember to completely clean up any accidents.

Separation Anxiety

Some dogs panic when left home alone. They may bark. They may go to the bathroom inside.

Some dogs don't like being left alone. You have to work with your new pet to get him used to being alone.

They may destroy walls, doors, or furniture. This is known as separation anxiety.

You can help get them used to being left alone. Try leaving for just a minute. Then try for two minutes. Slowly increase the times you leave. The dog will learn that when you leave, you also return. This may help.

Aggression

When a dog's bark sounds fierce, and he looks ready to bite or attack, this is aggression. Sometimes dogs act this way out of fear. Other times, they may react to other dogs, people, or around food.

Aggression is a serious problem. A dog trainer can help you find the cause and work with your dog to change his behavior.

Chapter 6
A Lifelong Responsibility

Dogs have been called man's best friend. That is because dogs are loyal companions. In return for food, shelter, and medical care, they give us so much.

Dogs can improve our mood. They can keep us from feeling lonely. They are always there to happily greet us when we come home. They snuggle with us. Dogs can even be good listeners. In these ways, they reduce stress. They help to make us happier people.

A Lifelong Responsibility

Dogs are also good for us in other ways. They get us moving when we pet or groom them. They get us outdoors exercising. They teach us responsibility. They give other people a reason to stop and talk. That may even help us make new friends.

Millions of Americans own dogs. Famous people now and throughout history have formed close relationships with them.

Dogs are great pets! You and your family can go for walks together.

President Dwight D. Eisenhower said, "The friendship of a dog is precious. It becomes even more so when one is so far removed from home. . . . I have a Scottie. In him I find

A Lifelong Responsibility

President Barack Obama and his family have a dog. Bo is a Portuguese water dog.

consolation and diversion . . . he is the 'one person' to whom I can talk without the conversation coming back to war."

Not only are dogs loved in the White House, but in Hollywood, too.

Comedian and actor Adam Sandler has an English bulldog named Matzoball. He interviewed the dog on *The David Letterman Show*.

Twin actors Dylan and Cole Sprouse also own a bulldog. His name is Bubba. They pose with him

Former president Harry S. Truman received Feller as a gift in 1947

fast facts

President Harry S. Truman owned a cocker spaniel named Feller and his daughter Margaret had an Irish setter named Mike. He once said, "If you want a friend in washington, get a dog."

for photos and play with him in their free time.

Singer and actress Hilary Duff owns a Chihuahua named Lola. Lola has her own blog on Hilary's Web site.

42

A Lifelong Responsibility

You can show your dog how much you love her, too. You do not have to be famous or have a Web site. Simply spend the time to care for your pet. Make a difference in your dog's life and you will have a friend.

Hilary Duff poses with her dog.

Spend time with your dog every day!

Glossary

aggression—An attack or other violent behavior.

agility—A sport where dogs compete on an obstacle course.

animal shelter—An organization that cares for homeless pets.

breed—A type of dog that came from a common ancestor.

crate—A cage used to house a dog.

groomer—A person who specializes in washing and cutting dogs' hair.

house-training—Teaching a dog to go to the bathroom outside of the house, also called housebreaking.

microchip—A computer chip ID that is injected under the skin of your dog, usually between the shoulder blades.

mixed breed—A dog that is a mix of two or more purebred dogs.

neutering—An operation on a male dog to prevent him from fathering puppies.

purebred—A breed of dog recognized by the American Kennel Club.

rescue group—A group that finds homes for needy and homeless animals.

separation anxiety—Fear that an animal has when he is left alone.

shedding—A natural process where hair falls out.

spaying—An operation on a female dog to prevent her from having puppies.

timid—Shy and scared.

traits—Characteristics that are inherited, such as blue eyes or the ability to see in the dark.

vaccines—Shots to prevent disease.

veterinarian (vet)—A doctor who takes care of animals.

Further Reading

Books

Bielakiewicz, Gerilyn J., Bethany Brown, and Christel A. Shea. *The Everything Dog Training and Tricks Book*. Avon, Mass.: Adams Media Corporation, 2002.

Coile, D. Caroline, Ph.D. *The Dog Breed Bible: Descriptions and Photos of Every Breed Recognized by the AKC*. Hauppauge, N.Y.: Barron's Educational Series, 2007.

Kalstone, Shirlee. *How to Housebreak Your Dog in 7 Days*. Revised edition. New York: Random House, Inc., 2004.

Patent, Dorothy Hinshaw. *Right Dog for the Job: Ira's Path from Service Dog to Guide Dog*. New York: Walker Books for Young Readers, 2004.

Further Reading

Internet Addresses

American Humane Association
<http://www.americanhumane.org>

Animal Planet—Pets
<http://animal.discovery.com/pet-planet/>

How to Love Your Dog: A Kid's Guide
to Dog Care
<http://loveyourdog.com>

Index